When Your Good
Just Ain't
Good Enough!

When Your Good

Just Ain't

Good Enough!

Written By:

MARY CLARK EUBANKS

ARPress
ILLUMINATING IDEAS,
EMPOWERING VOICES

ARPress
45 Dan Road Suite 5
Canton MA 02021

Hotline: 1(888) 821-0229
Fax: 1(508) 545-7580

Ordering Information:

Quantity sales. Special discounts are available on quantity purchases by corporations, associations, and others. For details, contact the publisher at the address above.

Printed in the United States of America.

ISBN-13:   Paperback   979-8-89389-134-8
                eBook   979-8-89389-133-1

Library of Congress Control Number: 2024911576

CONTENTS

· CHAPTER ONE ·

In the beginning God created the heaven and the earth. And the earth was without form, and void; and darkness was upon the face of the deep. And the Spirit of God moved upon the face of the waters.

Genesis 1:1-2 (KJV)

In the Beginning

GOD CREATED MAN IN HIS OWN IMAGE, in the image of God created he him; male and female created he them. Talking about being rated from the beginning, it was the time of inception. I was born feet first screaming and hollering as I entered this world. Yes, I was that grade, a "*breach*", they tell me. I guess, I thought, I was doing something, coming out feet first and ready to take over the world. But little did I know that the world was about to take over me. Sounds like I was getting ready to walk around and stir up some things. According to my late mother and many others, I did just that in so many ways. I was able to walk and talk myself in and out of almost anything. I was a loner but sometimes very outspoken at times and maybe too outspoken at other times if you know what I mean. I think that allotted me a lot of reservations about growing up. However, on the other hand, I have pondered on so many other circumstances in life as well that has caused me to wander and question my true individuality along with my purpose in life.

Growing up I always knew that the hands of God was upon my life and that God would use me in a special way. Anytime, someone in my home was going through an ordeal, I would hold their hands and encourage them that things would soon get better. I had a heart for God at an early age and I am happy that he trusted me and continues to do so. The bible talks about Purpose and being destined for Purpose. What do that really mean? Does it mean that at the beginning of time,

God already purposed our life to be what it is today? Does it mean that God himself pre-planned or pre-approved what and how you and I would thrive in this world? You must believe that God has a purpose and a plan for your life. You must know this, and grab hold to that one point alone knowing that his ultimate plan is for your good. It may not feel like it at this time that it is working for your good, but rest assure God is in control of your full destiny. He is the creator of life, the beginning, and the end. This lets me know, that regardless how things may feel or even look around me, I can take joy in knowing that Troubles may come, but they will not last. For, I am a strong believer, this too shall pass!

A very familiar scripture comes to mind:

For I know the plans, I have for you, declares the Lord, plans to prosper you and not to harm you, plans to give you hope and a future. *Jeremiah 29:11 (KJV)*

Even in knowing that, we have to totally Trust God in All His Ways that he will work things out for us in due time. Which means, he may not come when we necessarily want him to, but he is always on time. I know that sounds like a cliché but it is so true. We know that his timing is unlike our timing and when God shows up, he shows out, every time. I know that it is not always easy to have faith when we do not see the evidence of God's hands upon our life and our situation. But we have to trust God, even when we cannot trace him. Remember, Faith is not about what we can see, Faith is about what we cannot see. You must stand on that regardless of what anybody has to say or what you may be facing in your life at this moment. Falling prey to the enemy is exactly what the enemy wants and desires out of you at this time in your life. When you feel the most vulnerable is the time the enemy will attack you and hinder you from your purpose. For surely, the enemy will come in like a flood and try to overwhelm your spirit with grief and heartache and then torture you by making you feel that God is far away from you and your problems. You cannot turn back now and run like Forest Gump. You must STAND and declare in your walk that God Is and God Can regardless of what you may think you see. This thing is much bigger than you are anyway and far too much for you to try to handle on your own. But because I know that I serve a BIG God who can do BIG things in a BIG way, I look up to him to fix it like I know he can. This is the same God who is fighting on your behalf as we speak. This is the same God who spoke to David and gave him the power to slay Goliath by striking him in the forehead using a single stone. It was not by height or weight or even character, but it was by Faith that David was able to defeat Goliath and his army. David believed God would help him fight and be victorious against Goliath and the Philistines. You have to believe that God has your back, and he knows what to do in order for you to win in this battle of life. No matter what the situation in front of you may look like, just know God is in full control of it all. He is holding you up when you are weak and disheartened about life circumstances. You have to believe that God will never let you down because he is God, the Almighty, Jehovah Jireh, the provider. You have to believe that when you are at your lowest point, God is there with you holding you up making sure you don't fall. Sickness and Death is no match or competition for God. He is the creator of everything and everything is in his hands. Cancer, diabetes, and any other sickness cannot override God and his plans for your life. The words spoken over your life has to come to pass because the bible says that God's Word shall not return void. Every Word God has promised you and your loved ones have its own season, and we are just waiting on the rightful season for the harvest. And I believe without a doubt, it is harvesting time!

You must remember; we are talking about the same God who reminded Israel that he owns cattle on a thousand hills. With that said, I think, I can rest now and take a moment to give God the praise. All of this reminds me, I don't have to worry about anything and how I will make ends meet because they will meet with God's help. All I have to do is keep the faith and take all of my worries, my disappointments and all my concerns to the Lord and trust that he will work things out in my favor. God is the creator of life, and he knows what we stand in the need of before we ask. Who would not serve a God like this? He made the heaven and the earth along with you and me in his own image and then declared it was good. He made light and decided to divide the light from the darkness. He called the light Day and the darkness he called Night and then he said it was good. He begins to see the evening and the morning and called it the same day and said it was good. He took the firmament and the water and divided them and said that it was good. God is so fervent; he saw the dry land and called it Earth and the waters he called the Seas. God gave the sun, moon and the stars to preside over day and night and to mark the seasons, days and years and said that it was good. He created the fish and birds to fill the waters and the sky and marked that it was also good. Then God said, let the earth bring forth the living creature (animals) after his kind and everything that creeps upon the earth after his kind and God saw that it was good. On the seventh day, the bible said God rested and declared all that he had made to be very good.

God's days of creation can be a full lesson of its own. It identifies the strength of God and how he views us and everything that he has made. It is not by mistake that he has labeled us "good" because from the beginning his creating ability was so immaculate that everything he touched became "good". Man cannot comprehend the thoughts of God when he created us in his own image. The love of God took man and breathed life into us and made from us a representation of him although he knew we were not even worthy or more-less close to it. The more I meditate on the creation of the heaven and earth by the Almighty God, I am almost breathless. He saw me and you and then called it "Good". The worth that God sees in us when we don't even deserve it is mind-blowing to me. I only pray that I be able to see the good in others that God sees in me. I am always grateful and humble by his love for all mankind. So, this lets me know, In the beginning of my life, God's blueprint was already established and set for me to do His Will in which he had already declared "Good" and "Very Good".

Psalms 50:7-15 (NLT)

[7] "O my people, listen as I speak.
Here are my charges against you, O Israel:
I am God, your God!
[8] I have no complaint about your sacrifices
or the burnt offerings you constantly offer.
[9] But I do not need the bulls from your barns
or the goats from your pens.
[10] For all the animals of the forest are mine,
and I own the cattle on a thousand hills.
[11] I know every bird on the mountains,
and all the animals of the field are mine.
[12] If I were hungry, I would not tell you,
for all the world is mine and everything in it.
[13] Do I eat the meat of bulls?
Do I drink the blood of goats?
[14] Make thankfulness your sacrifice to God,
and keep the vows you made to the Most High.
[15] Then call on me when you are in trouble,
and I will rescue you,
and you will give me glory."

CHAPTER TWO

[38] For I am persuaded, that neither death, nor life, nor angels, nor principalities, nor powers, nor things present, nor things to come, [39] Nor height, nor depth, nor any other creature, shall be able to separate us from the love of God, which is in Christ Jesus our Lord.

Romans 8:38-39 (KJV)

Who Said It Would Be Easy

We as women have so much to deal with and it seems as everything, we strive to do is never good enough. Better yet, we as people alone have so much to overcome. Judging others is just the beginning of scrubbing the surface of it and holds a multitude of faults alone. Sometimes, I am so confused with life itself and don't know what to do at times. However, I do know, Giving Up is not an option. Although I tell you, it has definitely been ringing in my ears lately, but I know I got too much to lose in this fight. I understand the day-to-day task with working and taking care home can be challenging and Lord forbid if you are married and raising a family. Life itself can be very hard alone and adding any entity to it can be more demanding. Yes, I know sometimes we are often tied up with so much going on around us that we forget about the little things that are important to us. So, for women we tend to let ourselves go due to the expectations of others whether it be our spouses, children, jobs and the other responsibilities imposed upon us. It is the true nature of a woman to go the extra mile and neglect us in order to please others. However, we have to get to a place of serenity, not for others but especially for ourselves. Women are the ones who need to be refreshed and free from the everyday pressure of becoming "superwoman". As a woman, I am determined to move beyond the boundaries that are set up under a stressful and chaotic living pattern. I demand a platform that provides a peaceful and stress-free environment that will allow me to open myself up for solace and serenity. Where does it all end? Well, I think, I can answer that with one word that comes to mind…me! I have always been told that everything has a beginning and an ending. It is up to me to decide where I am going to get in and where I am going to get out. Even Jesus himself said that there was a time and season for everything, and a time to every purpose under the heaven. He also said on the seventh day he rested. This lets me know that he is aware that I cannot be everything to everyone just as well I cannot do everything for everyone. So, this is where the rubber meets the road. You have to learn to find balance and be able to set priorities on those things that you deem of most importance.

Sometimes we strive to be our very best and do the good to others that we feel is warranted and required. But, sometimes even in doing that, our good is not good enough. We either are accused of not doing enough or doing too much. Then all of a sudden, our self-esteem is being tested and we filter our way back to the same old place where we thought we were delivered from the beginning. We are judged on every hand about our appearance. Either we are too fat or too skinny. Point blank period. That is how we are viewed by many people in the world who only see beauty by looking through their "dark" tainted lenses. We are created in the image of God. He loves you and me for who we are to him, individually. He did not make two alike but different in so many ways which is the beauty of it all. We are able to walk in our own shoes, with our own shoelace and in our own shoe size. We are unique creatures, and we have to believe that and see that when we look in the mirror. God wants us to see what he sees in us when we look in our mirrors.

The bible says in Psalms 139:14, I praise thee; for I am fearfully and wonderfully made; marvelous are thy works: and that my soul knoweth right well.

God is not short concerning his promises and we have to know and believe that every word ever spoken from the beginning is his truth. I was reading an article earlier today and was reminded of the significance of this book. It resonates to me and hopefully to so many other people all over the world of different cultures and backgrounds. I feel it speaks to our spirit in so many ways and will help us find peace within our hearts and bridge the gap where there is a bleak and broken foundation. I know life is not always easy and no one has promised me a bed of roses and rainbow and lilies every day. But is it alright for me to dream beyond the expectations of this negative and impure atmosphere? I just want to be able to live life to God's fullest and not men. God has given me a promise through his Word that I am the head and not the tail, above and not beneath, a lender and not a borrower. That alone allows me to know that his Grace is sufficient, and I am overcome by the tactics of the enemy that tries to bind me in chains. God has freed me from every bondage and attack of the enemy that constantly tries to tear me down physically, emotionally, mentally, and spiritually. This is my testimony, and I am already overcome by it.

Sometimes, I sit and literally have to shake myself because of the things I often face. But I am content that my faith in God is not built on an unstable foundation. For I know that God is not finished with me yet and surely, he is not finished with you either. I don't care what comes my way or the things I may encounter that seems to want to take me out of here, I am determined to go all the way and see Jesus for myself. My full desire is to please God in all his ways. I am sure this will cause a lot of conflict at some point because that means someone will be short and it won't be God. I am a true believer that good deeds pay off in the long run, but you will have to keep focus regardless of the distractions. The bible speaks about fighting the good fight and finishing the course but overall holding on to your faith because at the end, that will be our test.

Recently, I have gone through one of the toughest ordeals of my life. I was talked about, criticized, and lied on but I still held on to my faith in God. Sometimes, it is hard to go on and hold your head up high when life deals you lemons. I know they said to make lemonade but at the time, I was not in the mood to cut up the lemons. I mean life can be hard by itself and adding such drama to the mix can be devastating. What makes it even harder is when it is family and people you love and respect. I had to take this matter to God in prayer and really see what God was speaking to me at the moment. Remember, when God allows suffering and pain to enter our lives it is for a reason. Those reasons can be anything as bringing you closer to him and/or preparing you for a new level in God. I really had to take a step back and seek God's guidance and see what he was speaking to my spirit. All I continued to hear him say is that I was closer to my breakthrough and all I had to do was to hold on and not let go. I believe God is saying the same thing to you as you read this book. Right now, God is preparing you for your next comeback and your next level in him. I know it don't feel like it and things look even worse than it did yesterday. But I want to encourage you to be steadfast unmovable and always abounding in the work of the Lord, knowing that your labor is not in vain. So, hold your head up and declare the blessings of God over your life. I made it and I know you can too! So, what, we struggled through and almost not made it. But they tell me, almost doesn't count. I am confident in knowing that although; I feel like giving up that I have to hold on to God's unchanging hands. I believe as it was said to King Jehoshaphat that this battle is not mines, but the Lord. Therefore, I will take courage and stand strong in my walk with God because I know that I am not alone.

James 1:1-10 (KJV)

James, a servant of God and of the Lord Jesus Christ, to the twelve tribes which are scattered abroad, Greeting. My brethren, count it all joy when ye fall into divers temptations, knowing this, that the trying of your faith worketh patience. But let patience have her perfect work, that ye may be perfect and entire, wanting nothing. If any of you lack wisdom, let him ask of God, that giveth to all men liberally, and upbraideth not; and it shall be given him. But let him ask in faith, nothing wavering. For he that wavereth is like a wave of the sea driven with the wind and tossed. For let not that man think that he shall receive any thing of the Lord. A double minded man is unstable in all his ways. Let the brother of low degree rejoice in that he is exalted: But the rick, in that he is made low: because as the flower of the grass he shall pass away.

CHAPTER THREE

Now unto him that is able to do exceedingly abundantly above all that we ask or think, according to the power that worketh in us, Unto him be glory in the church by Christ Jesus throughout all ages, world without end. Amen.

Ephesians 3:20-21 (KJV)

Even When It Don't Look Like It

"Life is like a box of chocolate, and you never know what you are going to get." I think Forest Gump was on to something here. Sometimes our view on life is different than others along with how we perceive a thing to be. I have found this out to be factual in so many aspects of my life, spiritually, emotionally, mentally, and physically. However, there is one thing that is rest assured and I take deep connection with God is God and he never changes. Regardless of what is happening around me and what it may look like, one thing is for sure, I have everything that I need because I have God. Now, I don't know about you but for me, there's nothing left to want when you have all you need. I am thankful for this gift and blessing that loves me despite all my wrong doings. God has never judged me or changed his mind about me, he just continues to love me unconditional over and over again. If anything, we are the ones who hit the gold mine if you are a believer. This is like having a savior to die for sins that did not belong to him or a savior speaking on your behalf when you have not even accepted him as your Lord and Savior over your life. We often seek God's guidance but sometimes we don't follow through on his examples. He lays out the road map for us, but we refuse to take his route and when the storm of life slaps us in the face, we run for a hiding place in him. We have to learn to trust God in spite of what it looks like. Yes, salt and sugar look alike but it does not taste alike. The sugar is sweet, and the salt is a bitter taste. But to see them both side by side will make you believe that they are the same. In saying that, we have to taste and see that the Lord who represents the sugar is good (sweet) and his mercy endures to all generation.

Having been saved at an early stage of my life has helped me understand the true value of relying on God for Help and watching him come through for me…every single time! Yes, even when I did not deserve it, he still showed up. Even when he knew I was not going to keep my promises to him, he still showed up. Surely, He, being God already knew that I would falter and fail him anyway, but he still showed up and on my behalf. Of course, it was not because I had done something so great and surely not because I was deserving of it, but because his humongous love for me and you that in spite of all of our wrongdoing, he forgives us, over and over again. Now, who would not serve a God like this?

There is one thing I have learned growing up as a little girl and that is regardless of what life may bring you to make the best out of it. It will get better sooner than later and/or by and by as I recall my dad would say. I have undergone "heart surgery" many times with people and the things they did to hurt me. Also, I had to forgive the many people who have not been sorry for the pain and hurt they have caused me. It is hard to forgive others when they have harmed you without a cause and they have no remorse. Peter asked God how often he should forgive his brother that sin against him. God told Peter to forgive not only seven times but until seventy times seven. This allows me to know that God wants a forgiving heart out of us. He desires to see us free from the pain and hurt caused by our enemies. We cannot allow the enemy to cause us to become bitter and hostile against others because of the pain they caused on us. That is why the bible says for us to forgive quickly. If we fail to forgive those who have wronged us, then God will not forgive us. Wow, sounds harsh, don't it? But it is not. Through all of this, God is teaching us His love for us and how it can change us on the inside if we follow his example. This is the same love he spoke about to his disciples and his other followers he met as he traveled the world. God desires us to have the same heart as he has for his people. We have to take the heart of God and allow it to change us through our walk, talk, and how we treat others, even our enemies.

Even in the midst of everything we encounter in life, God is still in charge, and he is working it out for us. All we have to do is stay rooted and grounded in him and in his truth by loving and respecting others. Sometimes our burdens can get heavy as we travel this path of life, but we must rest assure everyday will be like Sunday after a while. The days and weeks will be no more. The sickness and pain will no longer be a discomfort to our bodies anymore. There will be joy and peace and happiness that will reign all over us and consume our hearts. Oh, what a day of rejoicing it will be when we all get together and enjoy His everlasting peace and harmony. There will be no more hatred, lies, and deceitful attitudes because they will all cease and be no more.

One thing that I have to often remind myself, forgiveness is not about the other person but about me. Forgiveness is Freedom! I was reading this book the other day written by Bishop T.D. Jakes and he was saying that when we forgive others, they no longer have power over us. It is when we fail to forgive is when they hold power over us. After reading that over and over again, I begin to think to myself of how many times I have allowed people to control me with hatred and dislike due to my failure to forgive and forgive quickly. I will no longer allow this type of power to be given to anyone ever again. I know now that I have control over whom and what I give power to rule over my life. God has pre-destined me for greatness, and he has established my going in and my coming out. I do not have to worry about my enemies because they are already planted under my feet. I am not bound by the world and its views of me because I am mighty in God and in his sight. I have overcome the world, and his power has raised me up to trampled over them who rise up against me. We must declare and decree that we are mighty in God and in the power of His might. The bible has already reassured us that there are no weapons that are formed against us shall prosper and everything that rises up against us shall be condemned. Regardless, of what the enemy tries to say or do about that, he is a liar, and the blood of Jesus is already planted against him. So, let the church say Amen and Amen again!

Isaiah 54:14 (MSG)

"Just watch my servant blossom! Exalted, tall, head and shoulders above the crowd! But he didn't begin that way. At first everyone was appalled. He didn't even look human— a ruined face, disfigured past recognition. Nations all over the world will be in awe, taken aback, kings shocked into silence when they see him. For what was unheard of they'll see with their own eyes, what was unthinkable they'll have right before them."

CHAPTER FOUR

If my people, which are called by my name, shall humble themselves, and pray, and seek my face, and turn from their wicked ways; then will I hear from heaven, and will forgive their sin, and will heal their land.

2 Chronicles 7:14 (KJV)

Prayer Changes Things

As I sit here late past midnight reflecting on our world challenges with the numerous violent acts and crimes, I am devastated of the outcomes. It is really upsetting to watch my brothers and sisters next door be gunned down by people who vowed to protect and serve our country. In all of my life, I cannot remember anything more traumatic as this type of violence that has taken over America. If it was ever a time to pray, the time is now. I think that we have reached the maximal moment of truth that reveals that we cannot live safe in this world without prayer. It is time for America to wake up and get back into the game and pray. At this time, we cannot afford not to pray and lean on the everlasting arm of the almighty God. With the world being in this space, it is disturbing and if a change does not come soon, I am not sure what will happen next. I am 100% confident in the power of prayer and I know that prayer will change things. I have watched God change so many situations and circumstances in my life that is almost unbelievable. So, for me, I trust God with all my heart and all my mind and my entire soul for he is Jehovah-Shammah, the Lord is present.

Through the Word of God, I have learned not to lean on my own understanding but to acknowledge him in all my ways because I know he is in full control of my path. Regardless of what it may look like and how things may be slowly making turns, I believe God and I know he can heal our land. I am passionate about what I believe when it comes to God. I have seen God in a way that most people can only imagine and/or dream. I am a walking and living testimony with all the things and miracles God has performed in my life. I am in awe when I think of His Goodness knowing that I did not deserve it, but he gave it to me anyways. God saw fit for a little country girl from the south that people often overlooked and counted out and he blessed me beyond measures. I guess, he saw something in me that I sometimes don't see within myself and said that it was good. Talking about a second chance at life, the doctors told me years ago that I had a stroke and would never recover from the effects of it, but I did anyway. I am a miracle and a walking testimony, and I am grateful to God for his healing power and for doing it again and again. Every morning that I awake, I remind myself that the day is God's Day, and it is all in his hands whatever he may allow. I received a second chance to live a full and normal life. These days, I am not sure what to call "normal" anymore to be honest with you. Nothing almost feels "normal" with all the bad things that happen around us and to us. I just try to stay in my zone with prayer and keep my focus on him knowing that he is the purpose and focal point of everything surrounding my life. Prayer keeps me conditioned and prepared for the next test that will come my way and try to knock me off my post. But, because God reigns and I know that he reigns, I am committed in my way like Job, "Tho he slays me, yet will I trust him".

According to Google, Commitment is the state or quality of being dedicated to a cause, activity, or a person. It also says that Commitment involves dedicating and obligating yourself to something that can sometimes be large. As I pondered on the word Commitment, the words, Prayer, and Fasting come to mind. A lot of times, we fail to commit to a life of Fasting and Praying and then we wonder why our prayers are not reaching heaven's door and breaking up the folly grounds. We must become dedicated to the cause and seek God's guidance for his next move in our lives. And not this little clumsy five-minute prayer that we pray during a commercial break that we called so powerful and anointed. I believe that we think we have done something big when our prayer lasts a minute longer than the commercial. We are more in tuned to our favorite reality stars and movies than we are with our own reality. Do we really want to know what God think about us? Please, people, give me a break! And a much longer one than the prayer that you just prayed. We have become complacent and self-righteous, and we act as if we got it all figured out and worked out with our tickets in our hands ready to board the train. I must say, we are in for a rude of wakening if we don't get busy about God's business before the time is said it is too late. Like the song says, "I Pray We All Be Ready for His Return". I am not sure where you are in your life right now or how long you have been seeking God for answers. However, I want to encourage you and especially you to hold on to God's unchanging hands. Although, your situation may look dark and dreary and it seems that you have been waiting on your "time" for a long time now, Don't Give Up! The tests become harder when you are close to the finishing line. You have to believe that God's Word speaks life and life brings about a change in us. You cannot allow the enemy to hinder your purpose and limit your prayers. One reason the enemy wants to limit your prayers is because he has learned that your prayers will limit him. So, keep on praying and keep on fasting because your help is on the way.

I may have gone through many hardships in my life and some days, feel like throwing in the towel, but I refuse to give up on God. Of all the things I have battled with along my journey, God has never given up on me even when I gave up on myself. I cannot imagine my life without him, and I am happy to know that I don't have to. I often wonder how the unbelievers think things are working out for them. Do they realize that it is nothing but the Grace of God that allows us to even breathe and have our being? As I even write, I am shedding tears just thinking about his Mercy and Grace that he has over my life. I know that I am not worthy because I fail him daily and questions his plans for my life. People say that I should not question God, but I do. I don't mean to out of disrespect or anything, but I often find myself being curious and inquisitive about his creations. I also wonder why he takes so much out of me and you and still love us unconditionally. I mean, sometimes, I can be a hand full just like most of you. Yes. I am saved all day long, but I get in my feelings just like you do. The good thing is that he loves me no less than he loves you. Now, if that is not true love, I don't want to be right. This again, let us know that regardless of what man or anyone else sees in us, God sees the best and that alone is enough for me. So, after all, my Good still stands to be

Good enough. Thank You Jesus!

I have seen the hands of God on so many facets working in my life on so many occasions. There is no way that I can doubt God on any level. I mean, I have witnessed God to do the impossible things ever to happen that cannot be explained by man or woman. I am often amazed over and over of his unfailing love and adoration that he has for me. I remember a time that I was trusting God for some things to be granted to me on my job and before I could even get the prayer out of my mouth, it was already done. God is that type of God that will move when you least expect him to move. When he does it, it is always incredible to watch him work, and the results of his work can be astounding. I am pleased to know him and grateful for accepting him into my life when I did. Prayer is definitely the key, and it changes things beyond my wildest imaginations. But that is exactly who God is in our lives. He is indescribable and unspeakable and there is none other like him. Like the song said, I have searched all over and looked high and low and still can't find nobody greater than God. This is my testimony, and I am destined to tell the whole world about his goodness and his faithfulness. Throughout life, I have searched many outlets and people thinking that I could fill the empty places in my heart, but I found out that it was not possible. I later realized that the one and only thing that I needed was Jesus and until I received him and accepted him as my personal savior then and only then was, I filled and satisfied with the taste of his goodness. Mmm Mmm Good. We must learn to trust God and know that all things work together for the good of them who love God and are called according to his purpose. This is the Word of God, and it is true all by itself.

St. Matthew 6: 9-13 (KJV)

After this manner therefore pray ye: Our Father which art in heaven, Hallowed be thy name. Thy kingdom come, Thy will be done in earth, as it is in heaven. Give us this day our daily bread. And forgive us our debts, as we forgive our debtors. And lead us not into temptation, but deliver us from evil: For thine is the kingdom, and the power, and the glory, forever. Amen.

CHAPTER FIVE

^{9} Two are better than one; because they have a good reward for their labour. ^{10} For if they fall, the one will lift up his fellow: but woe to him that is alone when he falleth; for he hath not another to help him up. ^{11} Again, if two lie together, then they have heat: but how can one be warm alone? ^{12} And if one prevail against him, two shall withstand him; and a threefold cord is not quickly broken.

Ecclesiastes 4: 9-12 (KJV)

NOT EASILY BROKEN

Growing up in a large family was a little challenging for me. Having siblings who were older than I and having to be compared to them and their mistakes can be intimidating. Not to mention, growing up in a Christian home with a father who was a preacher and a mother who constantly stayed on her knees praying for her family. I was so blessed, but I don't think that I realized how much at the time. I was the one my family looked up to and depended on a lot, especially my parents. Sometimes, they portrayed me as "the perfect daughter". If you would have asked them, they would have said that they have no favorites. But in my eyes, I was their favorite child. I think I always had a way with my dad or better yet, he had a soft spot for me. He would give in quickly to my schemes. I believe, mainly because I seemed so fragile and appeared to be easily broken a lot of the time. I have always sensed he felt the need to provide me with more attention and care than the rest of my siblings because he felt that I needed it the most. As a child I stayed sick a lot because the doctors said early on that I had a heart murmur. I would often have these fainting spells where I would just black out. It happened most of the time when I would get tired and exhausted or too hot. At one time, we thought it was seizures but later learned that they were not. You better believe when the enemy can't get you one way, he's going after you in another way. However, I am grateful because I no longer must battle with those issues and concerns.

As I sit and think about my early childhood and having to deal with some of the health concerns, I experienced, I can only say "It was by your Grace and Mercy, God". I know that it was nobody but the Grace of God that kept me and healed my body repeatedly after my attacks. The enemy wanted to take me out so many times throughout my life, but God wouldn't allow him to. This allows me to know, God has great work for me to do and he is not finished with me yet. I believe this is the beginning of a lifetime for me. God protects what and who he has anointed and no matter what the enemy's plans is, God's plans are much bigger and higher, and they cannot be broken. This brings my attention to Job in the bible when the enemy went after Job to destroy his life; God limited the enemy's devices and wouldn't let him touch his life. Like Job, God has limited the enemy on how much and what he is allowed to do concerning you and me as well. Yes, I know the enemy desire to destroy us, but God has placed restrictions on the enemy and his plans. And today, I give him all the glory for just building a hedge of protection around me day by day as he always promised he would.

Growing up in a small pre-dominant white town in Georgia where people of color was often overlooked and marginalized, it was always important to know God. My family had strong ties in the black community because my daddy was a well-known preacher. Back then, everybody knew a preacher or wanted to know one at least. My sisters and I also sang on the gospel radio station every Sunday morning which also made us well known and liked in the community. We were often invited and travel a lot to visit churches both near and far to sing in which we really enjoyed. Most of the time, my mom and dad would make us coordinate our clothing and this would always make us feel important too. Our family values have always been strong and solid among each other. We were the cords tied together and that made us not easily broken. Don't get me wrong, we had our setbacks just like everyone else, but we refused to be defeated and allow the enemy to win at any cost. We held a strong bond in our family because we knew how to pray when things would get bad for us. I mean, talking about having to trust God when trouble strikes your home, faith was our key. My parents were the "Champions" when it came to putting forth our Faith and relying totally on God for guidance and support. People don't rely on their Faith as much as they did long ago. I remembered times when we would trust God for totally deliverance and healing of our loved ones. We didn't believe in waiting for a long time either before we had witnessed many times before the evidence of God's hands. We took God at his word when he said that all things are possible if we only believe so that is what we did, we believed. We expected God to show himself to us within that same hour or less because that is how we believed and was taught to believe. We were used to this type of move of God. There were no going to the hospital or going to counseling because we couldn't get it together. Don't get me wrong, with having a background (Master) in counseling myself; I believe that sometimes it is necessary and appropriate to go to counseling to help put things in perspective. But what I am talking about, people have lost their faith in God. Nobody wants to look to the hills from which cometh our help anymore. We immediately revert to what the doctors said and what they spoke over our lives. What about what God has spoken over your life and the promises he has made to you. What about the times, God came through for you when you didn't have any money to pay the bills or was late on the rent. We had no idea what we would do or what the bill collectors would do. But we put our trust in God knowing that he would work things out, right? Well, he is that same God right now! He is turning things around on your behalf just like he did for Job. God could have made so many decisions to deny Job, but he came to Job's rescue and today, he will come to your rescue. You must trust God in the midst of everything that you are going through no matter what it looks like. Some people put on their coats of faith only when things work out at the end. Well, so that you know, that is not faith. In Ephesians 11:1 it reads, Now, Faith is the substance of things hoped for and the evidence of things not seen. God has given us the power to call things to be. We must use the power within us to demand our bodies to be healed. We are powerful people, but we just don't know it or how to use it. We supposed to be kingdom minded people doing kingdom things and responding in a kingdom manner. The lame should be able to get up and walk after our intercessory prayers. The blind should open their eyes and see and declare the power of God's hands upon their lives. People should be eager to walk into the house of God and see God's hands and anointing upon God's people and witness the move of God. We should come EXPECTING the move of God and refuse to leave without seeing the power of his mighty hands. These things are not happening because we lack in our faith, and we deny the power within us.

I remember visiting a church one Sunday and I was so fragile and broken on the inside. I was going through an ordeal, and I could not shake the pain or the hurt. I got up that first Sunday morning feeling sad and depressed, but I was determined to make it to the house of God. I was so discouraged but felt if I could just get to the building or in the parking lot of the church that I would survive this thing. I thought if I made it to church that someone would see my pain and help pray me through my situation. I begin to think to myself, surely God has people who can discern in his churches, right? Well, I cried all the way to the church and walked in feeling somewhat hopeful that I would receive my breakthrough and deliverance. As the service moved along, I sat there hoping to be discerned, but nothing. I waited until the second part of the service and thought, surely the minister up preaching would see that I am hurting and pray for me. After the sermon, I walked to the altar and cried out for help and still nobody saw or discerned that I was deeply bruised on the inside. After I left church that afternoon, I asked God "How could anyone not see that I was broken and bruised" and I was crying out for help? God begin to reveal himself to me about our churches all over the world. Not just my church but your church too. He showed me that people in the churches today are not in-tune with his holy spirit anymore. There is a strong lack of anointing in the house of God. People are attending church and having church out of formality. We have a form of godliness that is not working for us, and we are denying the power thereof. There are so many types of formalities and rituals living going on in our churches and pastors are allowing it because they are afraid of losing members. We are no longer seeking God's guidance and leadership because we have lost our hope, our faith in the true meaning of worship and who God is. We rush through God's service, and we have an agenda that is unlike God's agenda because it is fleshy driven. People are over it and they are tired of the same old formality Sunday after Sunday. The same songs with the same message and no anointing are all too familiar and it has got to end somewhere. We must desire more of God and the things of God. Where is the move of God in our churches today? The bible says that we should be performing miracles as he did in the bible days. We should be walking in the power of healing the sick, and the lame should be able to walk after we declare God's healing over people. There is something wrong people and we must turn this train around because we are on the wrong tracks and headed in the wrong direction.

The bible talks about perilous times and how the world would begin to change drastically. People will begin to hate each other and seek to destroy others ferociously due to their devious behaviors and actions. These types of behaviors are happening around us right now with all the police killings and violence. It is just awful to turn on the television and watch the news and read the newspaper these days. Just sitting in the comfort of your home enjoying your family is dangerous and you never know how it will all end. It really alarms me on the inside when I think of all the violence and danger that lives next door to me. Somedays, I just want to cry and cry and cry because the world is at a loss and the people are headed for destruction. My answer to this whole massacre is that if it ever was a time to seek the Lord, the time would be now. God is still working in the miracle business and his blood still works and so does prayer. I am a believer in prayer and how it can change anyone and anything. Now is the time for people all over the world to just pray and seek God's face on what he is saying to us individually about the tragic going on around us. This world needs a corporate prayer and fasting and without it, I cannot see that we stand a chance to last long. As I continue to sit here, I can hear the words to this song that sounds like this: *What can wash away my sins? Nothing but the blood of Jesus. What can make me whole again? Nothing but the blood of Jesus. Oh, precious is the flow that makes me white as snow; no other fount I know. Nothing but the blood of Jesus.*

One thing, I will not do and that is give up and stop trusting God. For I am persuaded in my walk that nothing can separate me from God and his love for me. I am not easily broken, and I will continue to pray that you are not either. As the word tells us, Be Steadfast, unmovable, always abounding in the work of the Lord. No matter how difficult the road may seem, you have to believe that prayer is your answer to every situation that may knock on your door. Allow the Word of God to be your Comforter and find rest in Him and allow nothing to discourage you from your peace. Selah.

2 Timothy 3:1-7 (KJV)

This know also, that in the last days perilous times shall come. For men shall be lovers of their own selves, covetous, boasters, proud, blasphemers, disobedient to parents, unthankful, unholy, without natural affection, trucebreakers, false accusers, incontinent, fierce, despisers of those that are good. Traitors, heady, high-minded, lovers of pleasures more than lovers of God. Having a form of godliness, but denying the power thereof: from such turn away. For of this sort are they which creep into houses, and lead captive silly women laden with sins, led away with divers lusts. Ever learning, and never able to come to the knowledge of the truth.

CHAPTER SIX

Put on the whole armour of God, that ye may be able to stand against the wiles of the devil. For we wrestle not against flesh and blood, but against principalities, against powers, against the rulers of the darkness of this world, against spiritual wickedness in high places. Wherefore take unto you the whole armour of God that ye may be able to withstand in the evil day, and having done all, to stand. Stand therefore, having your loins girt about with truth, and having on the breastplate of righteousness.

Ephesians 6: 11-14

Giving Up Is Not An Option

Growing up in a large family, you had to be strong minded. I mean, you had to be stern and stand on what you believed or be taken down because of fear. Most of my siblings are older than I and I had to act tough even though I was not considered tough. However, I had to pretend to be to have my voice heard most of the time. Now, that may not be the way they saw it, but it was the way I felt during those times. At an earlier age, my dad had taught us the importance of saying what we mean and mean what we say. This was his philosophy in life, and he always held to that. I think my dad always felt the importance of being honest with people and expressing how he would feel about something and speaking on that without backing down. He has always been strong with words and actions to say the least. My dad was an authoritarian, and he took charge where he saw fit and felt no need of apologizing for it. I believe this made his preaching the gospel easier, because he did not back down when he was on the pulpit either. He would always say during his sermons that people don't like to hear him preach because he preached the truth and we know, people don't like the truth. I have found this to be evident and witnessed this so many times in my life that it is not funny.

In my family, we were brought up close and with a lot of odds against us because of what we did not have. But one thing that I will always remember my late mother telling us is that as long as we had God and each other, we had everything. Even when we did not have enough food to eat, she would not fear or doubt God. I have never seen anyone as strong as that woman, my mother. I would always watch her moaning and praying to the Lord and sooner than later somebody would stop by to bring us a bag of groceries. It was crazy to me because I did not understand the relationship she had with God. During that time, I did not have that type of faith in God and am not sure whether I knew God. I guess at that time, I was just too young and was only relying on my mother's faith. If there is one thing that I learned watching my parents go through their struggles of raising me and all my siblings that is their "Faith" in God. They did not waver but trusted that God would see us through and bring us out of the dark places. They always believed and instilled in us that Giving up, was never an option. I cannot remember a time when my parents ever gave up on God or said to us that they did not know what they would do to clothe and feed us when things got hard. Many times, I have watched my mother laboring before God all day without water or food. She would get up from prayer and study the bible and back down to pray. This is something that I do not see a lot of today. People are not willing to give up their food through fasting for the sake of others or even the sake of their own families. That is what I believe kept our family bond knitted so closely. The saying says a family that prays together stays together. And God knows we prayed and a lot. I can't remember how often we really played outside like children because we were really into church. For our fun times we played church at home. We would shout and dance in the dirt and afterwards my brothers would preach. Now, for us, that was our playing in the backyard. We were truly "preachers' kids".

There is one thing that I do remember that we did often and that is we would join hands in our living room and pray and pray until our eyes were red. I mean, we prayed a lot and to the point that I believed God knew each one of us by names. I think that we prayed about everything and even the cats and the dogs. Talking about someone who could get a prayer through to God, it was my parents. During those times, I think they really had a straight line in connection to God. Because when we would meet up in our living room to pray, about the time we finished praying and wiped our tears, our prayers were answered. I remember the doctors telling my parents that I had a heart murmur. I would have black outs and did not know why. I think that the doctors thought that I was maybe having fainting spells or seizures however, they were not sure. Of course, you know my parents did not claim any of that nonsense because prayer was our weapon and we believed in using our weapon. We believed God every time we prayed, and we expected him to show up and he always did. I think that is the problem in today's world, people don't expect God to show up. I mean, the bible has given us a road map and has taught us that God has to come through for us if we seek him diligently and by faith. Sometimes, I believe people pray just to hear themselves pray. Well, it is going to take much more than your words to get God's attention. He wants our hearts. He wants to know that when we pray our faith is strong enough to pull down the things of God. Prayer is and always has been my weapon and my strong tower. It doesn't matter what I go through in life, I still know that God is faithful. Now, I am not saying that in my faith walk, I do not get weak, and doubt does not creep in. What I am saying is that when I pray and things don't come to fruition, I still know that God can do it even if he decides now not to.

I was just thinking, where is this type of faith today? We stay so bound with our problems and stressed out and worried over what we don't think God is doing in our lives that we miss the move of God when he is doing it. It is time to get back to prayer. We have lost the unction in prayer and our faith is weak. We must stand against all odds of the enemy and whatever he brings our way. I know it gets hard sometimes and we feel like giving up and throwing in the towel. But I want to encourage you to hold on to everything you have to hold on to. At this moment and what you are going through, all your Help is right around the corner. You cannot give up so close to your breakthrough and miss the opportunity of a lifetime with God. It is time to suit up in your gear and put on the whole armor of God and watch God turn some things around on your behalf. It doesn't matter what the enemy has told you before you got in the fight, just know you have what it takes to win. You will not die but you will live. No demon, warlock, witch, or wizard can hinder the plans of God that has been spoken over your life. You must declare the blessings of God over your life and your family's life. Cancer and Diabetes cannot kill you and Jesus won't fail you. Prayer changes things. This is only the beginning of what God is about to do in you. So, hold on and don't let go because your healing is next door and it's calling your name.

What if God had given up on me when I gave up on myself? What if he had refused to die for a world that he didn't know and that didn't know him. What if he had rejected his father's request and refused to love us unconditionally and without judgment? Where will we be? Those imposed questions have me feeling queasy inside because I cannot imagine my life without God. He is everything to me and without him; I am nothing and can do nothing. Because of him I am who I am today and having him next to me is a feeling that is unexplainable. God is my deliverer and I often look up to him for guidance and support when things get too much for me to carry. I can never imagine a life without God especially when he is everything to me. He is my hope in sorrow and gives me peace about the woes of tomorrow. He constantly allows me to know that I am strong and undeniable, and I can do all things through him because he strengthens me. There is no one that can compete with him or hold his title because he is the one and only heavy weightlifter. He is my savior, my friend, my confident, my keeper, my strong tower and my redeemer and because he lives, I can live too.

Hebrews 10: 22-32 (KJV)

²² Let us draw near with a true heart in full assurance of faith, having our hearts sprinkled from an evil conscience, and our bodies washed with pure water. ²³ Let us hold fast the profession of our faith without wavering; (for he is faithful that promised;) ²⁴ And let us consider one another to provoke unto love and to good works: ²⁵ Not forsaking the assembling of ourselves together, as the manner of some is; but exhorting one another: and so much the more, as ye see the day approaching. ²⁶ For if we sin wilfully after that we have received the knowledge of the truth, there remaineth no more sacrifice for sins, ²⁷ But a certain fearful looking for of judgment and fiery indignation,

which shall devour the adversaries. [28] He that despised Moses' law died without mercy under two or three witnesses: [29] Of how much sorer punishment, suppose ye, shall he be thought worthy, who hath trodden underfoot the Son of God, and hath counted the blood of the covenant, wherewith he was sanctified, an unholy thing, and hath done despite unto the Spirit of grace? [30] For we know him that hath said, Vengeance belongeth unto me, I will recompense, saith the Lord. And again, The Lord shall judge his people. [31] It is a fearful thing to fall into the hands of the living God. [32] But call to remembrance the former days, in which, after ye were illuminated, ye endured a great fight of afflictions;

CHAPTER SEVEN

[16] So the last shall be first, and the first last: for many be called, but few chosen.

St. Matthew 20:16

I'm Next In Line

I GOT NEXT is what I continue to hear whispering in my ears as I lay here quietly and peaceful as the rain taps on my windowpane. Do you believe that you are next in line for a miracle? We have to believe that God will bring us through any problem that stands in our way. It does not matter what the intentions of the enemy, God is still able to bring us out. We must believe that there is nothing too hard for our God. If he brings us to any situation, he can bring us through it. As I write this chapter, I am reminded of a vision that God showed me a couple of years ago. I saw a long line of people and the line was so long that I could not see the end of the line. There was a clear door at the front where people were standing and there hung on the door a red and white round cardboard paper made of a clock. The sign read "Will Return". There was a time noted on the cardboard clock. I begin to see the people standing in line talking among themselves wondering will anyone return. As I saw myself walking out of the door where the clock hung, I begin to hear God say to me "Please Come Back". Then as I kept walking, God showed me this revelation as to what will happen if I did not return. He began to tell me that there are gifts and the anointing planted on the inside of me to call things in people's life to flee and it shall flee. He said that I had to come back and give the people what he had stored in me. He began to say that the people's life was in my hand and that if I did not return that the people would become discourage and turn back from God. I begin to weep and moan as God showed me in a vision of so many people's soul that was standing in that line. I saw all types of people from every race and ethnic groups and background. They were waiting for an impartation from me to give to them. Oh boy, I was amazed and stunned of the wide range of people all over the world waiting to be endowed with the anointing that God himself had entrusted in me.

There are many people who God has anointed and ordained to do just the same, to impart in other people. We fail God when we disown his callings and deny his word to his people. It is time out for our long-drawn-out excuses on why we cannot be more available for God. All God wants from us is a yes to do his will. He has been and is more than we could ever imagine he could be in our lives, but we continue to dishonor his love for us. I am ashamed of my own shortcomings and pray for a more obedient heart that is willing to give up my selfish ways and pick up my cross to follow Jesus. Out of all the things we have done in our lives, God still chose us to be a part of his plan. No matter what the enemy will try to do to destroy God's plan, he can't because God's favor has already placed a marked that cannot be erased. For that, I am very grateful, and I believe that we are next in line for a miracle.

How many of you have participated in an event and your whole intention was to succeed and maybe to win it? Maybe it was succeeding in a game, passing a major test, and/or accomplishing a major life goal and you were determined. Again, you put forth good effort, self-control, discipline, and motivation. You studied hard and stayed focused on the task at hand. You refrained from complaining and pushed yourself even when others tried to discourage your walk. You labored, prayed on it, fasted, cut the carbs, ran, and even gave up bread and counted every single calorie intake daily. But out of all that hard work you still failed! You still lost the game, failed the test, didn't get the loan, didn't lose the weight, couldn't have that baby, and still didn't succeed in that relationship and you were devastated.

Have you ever been in a situation where it seems like nothing you do is ever good enough You bought the groceries, paid the bills, put the kids to bed early, cleaned the house, mowed the lawn, did the laundry, cooked dinner, and even baked a cake but still it was not good enough. The kids are still complaining, husband is still grumbling, employer is still not happy, and even the dog/cat is disgruntled and whining. And you just feel like throwing up your hands and walking away from it all. You prayed about, fasted, and stayed in your Word; however, things had not changed and now you were beginning to get discouraged. And there you sit in the face of God and asking "Lord, How Did I Get Here!" I want to encourage you that God has not forgotten about you. The wind may blow ten times harder than it did yesterday but there is nothing that can stop the hands of God on your life right now. Your deliverance is right around the corner, and it has your fingerprints and your DNA. So, there is nothing the enemy can do to screw this up now. His time has run out and now it all lay in the hands of God. The one who has all power to rectify and over-turn your situation as we speak. Plus, you cannot turn back now because you are up next. God has pulled your ticket, and your name is printed on the board and all you have to do now is answer the call.

There are times when we feel it is impossible to move forward because the enemy has beaten and tortured our self-esteem. We do not believe that we are good enough to be loved by anyone including our own family and friends. Our marriages are in a dilemma and our children are out of control with the letters D.I.S.R.E.S.P.E.C.T. Our neighborhoods are polluted and infested with sex, crimes, drugs, and prostitution. There are no jobs and very little income, and people are losing their heads because they are unable to provide for their families. At this point, the world itself is in a phase that is questionable and uncertain. Overall, it is challenging and very hard to move on as it seems almost impossible to expect change and be the change as our former President Barack Obama likes to remind us. But then I remember who I am in God and what God is in me and that makes the world of a difference, and it brings me peace. We cannot allow ourselves to be brought down and measured by the deeds of this world. Yes, we are in a fight and the battle is not over until God says that it is over. We have to remember that this fight we are in is Spiritual. You are not my enemy, and I am not against you. It is the devil and his amps that I am targeting. The enemy will try to make you believe that your own family, church family, and close friends are your enemies. Well, I beg the difference. I may struggle to understand some of the things that I may encounter with my family and friends, but I know that at the end of the day, it is the enemy who has brought the negative seed and planted it. Can you see who the real culprit here is! The enemy desire for us to always be in conflict among one another. This is so that we can become so distracted with everything else going on around us that we ignore his temptations and antics to destroy us. Again, you are not my enemy! Remember in the bible, God told King Jehoshaphat in 2 Chronicles 20th chapter that although they were in a fight that the battle was not even theirs but the Lord. God wants to remind us today to depend on him and not on our own understanding. We must stop trying to fix everything and everybody especially when God has not offered your help. Sometimes, you just have to sit in your situations and believe what's coming is better than what's been. We must believe that God can handle our problems much better than we can ever handle them if we let him. It is time for us to relinquish all control to the Lord no matter what the enemy brings our way. We must stand in agreement with Ephesians 6:12 that say: "For we wrestle not against flesh and blood, but against principalities, against powers, against the rulers of the darkness of this world, against spiritual wickedness in high places."

It is inevitable that the enemy will show up and pressed his way through to discourage and dishearten God's people, but we must be in tune with the Holy Spirit that tells us to go ahead and not doubt the hands of God. I can admit there are some things in my own life that needs adjusting and I confess to them now because I realize although the enemy chases me, God has begun a good work in me, and he promised to complete it. We must believe that although it seems as if we are always coming up in the rear, God has already sacrificed his life that will allow us to receive and benefit from the first fruits of our labor. I agree that all we have to do now is to abide by the Word of God that says, "Be ye steadfast, unmovable, always abounding in the works of the Lord for we know that our labour is not in vain". No matter what may come our way, to deter us and cause us to become weak and weary, we must hold on to God's unchanging hands and know that soon we will be done with the troubles of this world. And after all of this is over, we are going to our heavenly home where we can settle down and rest to enjoy the feast of the Lord forever and ever.

About a year ago, I remember going through a touch patch in my life and I wanted to throw my hands up and quit. Someone very close to me encouraged me by reminding me that the closer I get to my breakthrough that the storm would get stronger. They even went on to say that people that I thought was in my corner and cheering me on would no longer be there. They would all have walked away because of the turbulence and disturbance that storms can sometimes bring. I begin to talk to God, I felt somewhat like Joseph when he was going through his struggles and calamities. Joseph couldn't understand why he was thrown in the pit, but he believed God and his word. He believed that God would come and rescue him and bring about justice. This is exactly what you must do during this low time in your life. I asked God time and time again "Why"? I could not understand my feelings nevertheless explain it to anyone else at the time. Although I knew deep down that God was still God and that he would come to see about me. The pain was evident, and the tears were real, but I refused to give up and turn my back on God. So, instead I begin to pray and fast and seek God daily for answers to my problems so that I could better understand his plan for my life. It was amazing and happened in the middle of the night as God appeared before me to provide me with directions as he instructed me to go forward and not look back. Enthusiasm leaped over me, and I begin to see my life as God sees it. I am no longer bound to this world because I understand that the combination to my praise is not my struggles or how I view them but how I am overcome by them. My praise is what continues to push me into my next level and that is why I cannot afford to get distracted. We must realize that our praise is our weapon and that is why the enemy continues to fight after it. The enemy knows that our praise is the cornerstone to our victory. I am persuaded, I am next in line and there is nothing that the enemy can do about it.

Deuteronomy 20:1-4 (KJV)

When thou goest out to battle against thine enemies, and seest horses, and chariots, and a people more than thou, be not afraid of them: for the LORD thy God is with thee, which brought thee up out of the land of Egypt. ² And it shall be, when ye are come nigh unto the battle, that the priest shall approach and speak unto the people, ³ And shall say unto them, Hear, O Israel, ye approach this day unto battle against your enemies: let not your hearts faint, fear not, and do not tremble, neither be ye terrified because of them; ⁴ For the LORD your God is he that goeth with you, to fight for you against your enemies, to save you.

CHAPTER EIGHT

[7] Beloved, let us love one another: for love is of God; and every one that loveth is born of God, and knoweth God. [8] He that loveth not knoweth not God; for God is love.

I John 4: 7-8

A Love That Never Quits

For God so loved the world, that he gave his only begotten Son, that whosoever believeth in him should not perish, but have everlasting life. It never fails me how much you can love something and someone so bad that it hurts. And I am thankful for the love that God gives us that overwhelms our hearts and mind to be able to love and be loved. I am always amazed of his love for me especially when I know that I am undeserving and unfit of his graciousness, but he loves me anyway. Now that is a point blank and period. Which means there is nothing else need to be said after that. He so loves me regardless of my circumstances and even my flaws. My God is still in love with me. Yes, with all of my shortcomings, attitudes and inadequacies. Not that I deserve any of it because I really don't but his love for me is pure and untainted. Some say a glass of water can be lasting, but I beg the difference. When you get a sip of the Love that only God can give then you have found an 'everlasting love" and that is a love that won't quit.

To Love God Is to Know God. I had to really think about that and found it to be so true. God chose me to be his and I in return chooses him daily to be mine. This is a love story between Jesus and me. When I begin to look over my life and see how many times God has protected and sheltered me from danger seen and unseen, I am in awe of his love for me. I remember some of the selfish and unkind things I have said and done not only to myself, but others as well. And oh, don't mention how ugly and ungrateful I have acted when I did not get the things I wanted from him. Oh boy, I know he really had to dig deep with me and pray to his father. You know how people can get when they don't get what they want and when they want it. And don't you dare think for a second that you can love anyone more than God loves you. His love for us was shown by him dying on the cross for our sin and there is no comparison in all the earth. He died for a world that was weak and wicked and where he committed no sin and had no fault. He died for a world that lied and denied him all in the same day. Not to mention the stones they threw at him and all of the hurtful and awful words they called my Lord. They tried to discredit him, but they couldn't because his father had already prayed and prepared him for the journey and for that, To God Be the Glory!

When I think about it, God loves you and me more than we could ever be loved in our whole lifetime. Now, that is true LOVE that never quits! I have made a whole lot of errors in my life that was not pleasing unto God but every day he continues to wake me up again and again. Why? For one, because this is the love of a father who love his child. You see when you love it is unconditional. Which means, there are no conditions and no cost to it. Love is Free. So, if you are in a place where you feel that you have done the unforgiveable and the worst sin possible. I want to let you know that I know a God that sits high on the throne and looks down low that love you despite all your mess. You must remember that you will never see God if you never experience pain and suffering. Believe it or not, it is a part of God's plan. Whether you are bound in prison in your mind or a physical location, just know, you can be redeemed and there is Hope. It doesn't matter what the enemy has told you and tried to make you believe. Be Encourage and know that God has not forgotten about you. He is there to protect and keep you from all that comes to destroy your mind. You have to believe; it is not over for you. Well, it is over for him, and he knows it too which is why he continues to pursue you. You see, he was kicked out of heaven because he became too arrogant with a takeover spirit that God was not allowing in his camp. He wanted to tell God what to do and how to do it. So, because of his hostile ways and deceitfulness, the enemy was no longer allowed to discourage anyone else ever again. Therefore, he was then casted into hell where he would rule and reign forever. I am thankful to God for his love to shield us from all the harm and the danger of this world. He keeps on blessing me over and over again and I am so privileged to be called one of his children.

I have seen so much in my lifetime and have experienced so much hurt and pain that is overwhelming. I have cried myself to sleep many days and nights haunted by the thought of harming myself because of what the enemy had planted in my head to believe at the time. There was one point and time in my life I almost lost my mind because the pain was too unbearable. Having your virginity taken from you and feeling disgusted and with guilt all at the same time can be overwhelming for a young teenager. How about not being able to tell anybody because you are too afraid and fearful of being judged by everyone. Not to mention the abuse both physically and mentally. But you feel compelled to keep that a secret although that would make you feel even more helpless. You already feel alone and lost like a stray puppy with no belongings. But when I tell you that there is **total healing** that only comes from God himself that can put you back together again. This is a part of God's plan for your life. He wants us to be able to trust him with the most sensitive and intimate details of our lives. He has expressed his love and grace to us time after time. All we have to do is to embrace his love and gentleness and allow him to do what he has come to do and that is Love us unconditionally.

During these hard times, I remember trying to push God away because I felt unworthy and undeserving of his love. The more I pushed him away, the closer he came to me and wrapped his arms around me. Oh, the Love that I felt was indescribable because I had never felt that type of love in my life. The love of God could never be measured. It was warm, kind, gentle and peaceful all at once. I felt so much love and joy that day like I never felt before and from that very day my heart was strengthened. I was able to open myself up to love others and allow others to love me in return and without the guilt. I have searched this life over and over and still cannot find another being that gives me the chills and thrills that God himself gives me every day of my life. I know that I am not deserving but does it matter? God saw a broken soul and he had compassion for me and mended my torn heart in order for him to use it for *His* good. For that, I am humbled by his love forever.

One day, I remember thinking to myself "Who could love a sinner like me?" I was born into this world to be a part of a generation that was expected to love and be loved. However, my love was taken away from me on one hand and beaten out of me on the other. I was tormented in my mind everyday having to deal with the hurt and pain that I was experiencing. I thought I was going to lose my mind and I probably would have if it had not been from the Lord who was on my side. At one time in my life, I trusted in love and thought that it would cover me but somewhere I lost faith in the true love that I longed for. Sometimes when the love you have becomes polluted and is snatched away from you without warning, it can be very detrimental and damaging to your soul. But I have learned that the Almighty God is able to do exceedingly, abundantly above all that we may ask or think. Even when I wanted to give up and walk away from the only true love, I know which is Jesus the Christ, he would not let me go. He carried me when I became weak and feeble and no longer wanted to finish the course. He pitied me and gave me a place where I could lay my head and rely on him for the strength and support that I needed to endure through my hard times. Out of all the many times I have let God down, He has never failed me once. His love is contagious and because of it, I have learned to trust in Jesus, and I have learned to trust in God and through it all.

The love of Jesus always seems to protect me even when I am underserving and is without justification and that my friend is called Grace. What is Grace? Grace is God's undeserved, unearned, and unmerited favor. Grace is the unconditional love that is given to us although we are not deserving. His love, through Grace is empowering and selfless on every level. And without God's favor, I know without a doubt that I would not be here today to share my encounters and life story with you. God's Grace is sufficient and abundant. It is because of his Grace that you and I are still here today and are gifted to maintain the standards of the Lord. I am forever grateful of the Grace and Mercy that God continues to bestow upon us without measure. My friend, there are no big and little sins. They are all equal in the sight of God because sin is sin regardless of the extent of it. It is time to abolish sin and allow God to cleanse our mind, body, and soul of the toxic waste that the enemy has brought to destroy us. It is now, where we have to use the power within us to cast down every foul spirit and every foul word that has ever been spoken over our lives. We have to believe that God is strongest power, and we are not defeated no matter how bad the enemy talks and brings us fear. We are strong in the Lord, and we have to go and declare and decree that on today. The devil is a liar if he thinks that I am about to give up when I am closer today than I was yesterday to my deliverance and my breakthrough. The Word of God encourages me that when I am weak, God is strong. His unconditional love and affection pursue me and guards me from the danger that attempts to conquer me.

This morning, I awakened and had to smile because I realized that last night I slept with Grace. God's Grace. God continues to show his love for me every morning that I open my eyes. His love is everlasting, and his strength is never ending. But his Grace is sufficient, and I am enthused of his endearment and sacrifice for me. Sometimes, I sit and think of God's goodness and his love for you and I and I am amazed. He has shown himself to be a father, mother, sister, brother, and a friend and so much more. He has not ever let me down and/or been short concerning his promises to me. I am forever thankful of his presence each time he makes himself known to me and hover over me with his spirit. Oh, how I look forward to commune with him daily and sit at his feet to embrace his power and glory. His Mercy and Grace is endless and sets no boundaries upon me as I worship him. I am often captivated of God's continued Grace and Love that works for us, in us, and through us. For that, I am in such a peaceful and serene place because after all I have been through; I am able to finally acknowledge and embrace the love within me. Time and time again, I am often overwhelmed by his spirit and filled with his joy, the unspeakable joy. Now that is a Love that just won't quit.

I Corinthians 2:9-10 (KJV)

But as if is written, Eye hath not seen, nor ear heard, neither have entered into the heart of man, the things which God hath prepared for them that love him. But God hath revealed them unto us by his Spirit: for the Spirit searcheth all things, yea, the deep things of God.

CHAPTER NINE

Who shall separate us from the love of Christ? Shall tribulation, or distress, or persecution, or famine, or nakedness, or danger, or sword? As it is written, "For your sake we are being killed all the day long; we are regarded as sheep to be slaughtered." No, in all these things we are more than conquerors through him who loved us. For I am sure that neither death nor life, nor angels nor rulers, nor things present nor things to come, nor powers, nor height nor depth, nor anything else in all creation, will be able to separate us from the love of God in Christ Jesus our Lord.

Romans 8:35-39

I'm Determined

Do I have any honest people who can attest with me that they have lived in a season of their life where they have felt hopeless, helpless, disappointed, desperate, depressed, and simply frustrated with life and everything that comes with it? The job, family, finances, church, and friends became almost too much to deal with and you felt disheartened. Yes, I am a believer and I trust in God's Word. I know that God can do anything but fail, but at the beginning and the ending of my day, sometimes reality sets in and I become discouraged in my walk. I know sometimes people think once you get saved that people are exempt from troubles and temptations. Well, to be honest with you, it is the opposite. I personally feel that temptations and oppositions are more prone to happen once you give your life to God. Because remember, the enemy wants and goes after what he knows he cannot have. The enemy pursues the ones who are gifted and anointed with the Power of God. The enemy don't care about you and me. Remember, this is the same devil who was kicked out of heaven for his aggressive behaviors by trying to tempt God and tell him what to do. Surely, he is still manipulative and desire for you and I to side with him and become a non-believer in the Most Holy God as well. The devil is not afraid of you because you are no threat to him. We are so passive and submissive to the devil when he tries to steal our peace and joy that it has now become so easy for him. I no longer believe he takes our peace but rather we give it to him and without a fight. I am tired of getting out of bed tired and going to bed tired because the enemy keeps fighting me in my thoughts and dreams. The bible says for us to use the scriptures, the Word of God to ward off the enemy. We have to cast these perverted thoughts and spirits down. If we want to combat the enemy, we must be ready to go head-to-head and rebuke every foul spirit that comes against us to steal our peace and joy. We have the power to declare and decree God's Word over our family and loved ones without any hesitancy.

A friend texted me today and said that he had been getting in a lot of fights in his dreams lately and he didn't understand why. He then said that the last dream he had the night before was a dream of him fighting someone with a knife. I immediately texted him back and instructed him to pray but with authority and power to cast down those thoughts that the enemy tried to plant. We have to be aggressive with the enemy because he already thinks that we are weak and pathetic when it comes to fighting for what belongs to us. There is a song that is sang by Karen Clark Sheard that says, "Everything that the Devil Stole God is Giving it Back to Me". Now, I have heard some of you say, you don't want your old stuff back. Okay, I hear you and now hear me. I want everything that the devil stole from me and the new stuff that God has already pre-ordained for my life. I know some of you may not agree with me on that, but that is okay too. I'm just saying. We can agree to disagree on this one. You have to remember what the enemy stole wasn't his from the beginning. Therefore, I am breaking down his camp with all his imps and I am declaring and decreeing a *"lose"* of all my stuff back. Once I get my stuff he stole back, even if I no longer use them, I still want it back. It is time for us to go in on *war* mode with the devil. It is apparent, God knew we would be in a war with the enemy which is why he encouraged us to suit up in our gear. In Ephesians 6:11 the word tells us to put on the whole armor of God that you may be able to stand against the schemes of the devil. God already knew that the enemy would not fight fair, so he warned us to be ready and girded and entangled with the truth for us to withstand.

I know that things can get very difficult at times, but I am not at a place where I can just quit and give up on God. I AM DETERMINED TO GO ALL THE WAY. Out of all the things I have been through and continue to go through in my life, God has been nothing but faithful to me. Now, I have experienced some close encounters where I have had major tests with health issues and concerns, but God has always been consistent with his unfailing love through it all. God has always brought me out on top and allowed the twins, Grace, and Mercy to overshadow my life with his substance that seems to bring me through. I will endure and fight as long as I have breath in my body to do so. Life can be challenging and the thought of simply letting go is just a thought. Like you, I have experienced so many ups and downs to the point of me not wanting to catch my next breath. But then I remember, *"The Cross"* where he died for me and you and through all the torture and pain that he endured, the bible said that he *never* said a mumbling word. I remember when I was a teenager, I would go to my mother and complain about my problems, and she would say "You do know some people are having it much worse off than you right now?" I would walk away thinking they must not live in this city because I haven't met them yet. At the time, it seems like I was the only one going through what I was going through, and it was bigger than earth. Being in a place of solitude can be heart wrenching, not feeling loved and like you do not belong. Sometimes, you can be a part of something or someone's life and still feel disconnected. Isolation is a feeling that follows you wherever you go, and it seems to haunt you from place to place. Often, a person heart can ache so much that it begins to physically hurt. Loneliness is a disease that fights people and tear at their hearts until it stops pumping for air. Inhale, Exhale is what I am often reminded as I try to keep my sanity along with staying conscious of everything around me. Who wants to be in a place where it seems like you just exist but are not important to anyone? They say, blood is thicker than water, but is it? Determination says that I can do all things through Christ that strengthens me. Determination says that I can establish anything with a positive and a never give up attitude. Determination gives me the power to push under odd and abnormal circumstances even when I question my own ability to sustain. God has given me the strength that I need to fight and stand as I uphold the blood stain banner in spite of the enemy's plans for my life. That blood was not my families but God himself, the Great, I AM. I am forever Grateful for his blood that shed on Calvary cross just for me and you. I am more convinced now than ever; the blood still works!

I know that life is worth living and I am grateful to God for my life. The Word tells me to, count it all joy when I fall into various temptations that my faith will not fail me but find patience in the works of the Lord. I know that God has not brought me this far to leave me but to carry me through every obstacle that comes to make me quit. I know that to quit is not an option for me and I no longer loiter with the mindset of failing. The enemy has a way of making you feel isolated and secluded from the ones you love and the ones that love you. By doing this, he creates a way in and a way out of your life without any roadblocks contrary to his plans. But fret not, God has not given you a spirit of Fear but of the power to conquer every attack of the enemy. Always remember this the "Greater" that lies within you has the authority to slay every untamed and wild foe of the enemy that tries to step foot on the campground only authorized for you and your family. I want you to repeat this over and over again until you get it in your spirit and begin to believe it. Again, I remind you to be determined to go all the way whether in rain, sleek or snow. Today, I am convinced that I am safeguarded and strapped for my next course for I know that it comes without a prize but with a price. However, I am good with the cost because I am completely sold out and committed to serving in my next position. I trust God with all my heart, and I believe, come the finish line lies a cross just for me and I will pick up my cross and follow Jesus.

There are some things you can rest assure in God and that is Love, Peace, Joy, and Longsuffering. These ingredients will always be a form of evidence to a full life and righteous living that will allow you to be conditioned for what is coming next. God's love is pure and everlasting, and he cares for you and only want what is best for you. Sometimes we can get stuck in one place because of being too comfortable in a situation. I believe that sometimes we do not have the faith and assurance of God's Word that all things work together for the good of them who love God and are called according to his purpose. I truly believe that God want us to push beyond every obstacle and situation that tend to place limits on us. We have to believe God and know that he will meet our every need just as his Word has spoken. In Philippians 4:19 it encourages us: But my God shall supply all your need according to his riches and glory by Christ Jesus. His word has promised us this and all we have to do now is to sit back and relax and wait in expectations that the Word of God will come to fruition.

Recently, I had a conversation with this young lady who looked very fragile, and she appeared to be at her wits end. She didn't know what to do or how to get out of her situation. She seemed to me to be in a state of depression, and she made that very clear during our conversation. Her one liner over and over again to me was *"I just can't take no more"*. How many of us have been there? Where life has taken you down a dark and dreary road and you felt lost and abandoned. You tried and reached out to your family and friends, but they seem pre-occupied and distant at the time. You tell yourself that giving up is your last resort, but down on the inside you knew that wasn't true either. Guilt rode your emotions because you knew that the bible tells us that he will never leave us nor forsake us. Although at the time, you were not feeling that and only sought a hiding place where you could hide and bury all of your woes. You continued to seek God for answers but there is none given. Now, you become frustrated and almost at a breaking point where you are about to surrender to the pain, hurt and guilt and just let go. Then suddenly out of nowhere you are reminded through a text message that God is the strongest power and because he is, you are not defeated.

I am over the youth department at my church, and I really enjoy speaking with different youths and youth groups. Often, I like to remind them on how easy it is to give up. Anybody can give up and walk away from their assignment and never look back. It is a challenge to be steadfast and unmovable in anything that you strive to do in life. Now, this is where the rubber meets the road. Are you conditioned to suffer for the sake of Christ in a time of disaster and when all the odds are against you? Because sometimes you will experience life major turbulence that will push you to the edge and then sweep you off your feet. I will say it like this, you better make sure that you have J.E.S.U.S. on speed dial because you will need him and every step of the way. But the good news is that God will never put more on us than what we can bear. I am a witness that I have suffered great pain in my life, but God has piloted me through every one of them. His love has resuscitated me back to life so many times when I was drowning in life troubles and dilemmas. I wanted to even die at one point in my life, but God had other plans for me, and he didn't allow the enemy to take me out. The order that the enemy conjure up for me was cancelled and abolished from the root. I am so glad that I came to know Jesus for myself and now I am more determined than ever and there is no looking back.

I Corinthians 9: 22-27

[22] To the weak became I as weak, that I might gain the weak: I am made all things to all men, that I might by all means save some. [23] And this I do for the gospel's sake, that I might be partaker thereof with you. [24] Know ye not that they which run in a race run all, but one receiveth the prize? So run, that ye may obtain. [25] And every man that striveth for the mastery is temperate in all things. Now they do it to obtain a corruptible crown; but we an incorruptible. [26] I therefore so run, not as uncertainly; so fight I, not as one that beateth the air: [27] But I keep under my body, and bring it into subjection: lest that by any means, when I have preached to others, I myself should be a castaway.

CHAPTER TEN

When you lie down, you will not be afraid; When you lie down, your sleep will be sweet.

Proverbs 3:24

Pray without Ceasing

Now I lay me down to sleep, I pray the Lord my soul to keep; If I die before I wake, I pray the Lord my soul to take. Amen. This is a prayer that I prayed as a little girl every night before I went to bed. Growing up in a Christian home, we believed in prayer. One thing my family taught me is how to pray and the importance of prayer. We prayed a lot and that is what was expected of us. Because of the way we were taught in our home, prayer was an antidote for all our problems. Our Faith was very strong, and we believed God and his Word. So, we sought God often and not because we were told to, we believed in God and what he could do because we had seen him perform so many miracles in our home on many occasions. Praying for us was like our daily bath. It was something expected and normal for us. That's why I don't understand why people can say that they forgot to pray during the day. To this day, I cannot imagine going a day much less than for hours without praying or just talking to God. My parents taught me and my siblings that prayer is what gets us through our everyday storms. I believed that back then when I was a little girl and I still feel the same today. Prayer is the key to any unlock door. I know the bible says, pray without ceasing, and I truly believe my parents won the grand prize on that one. My mother would always remind us that the more we seek God the more he would recognize our voices and answer our prayers when we called on him. I always wanted God to know my voice and I studied him in his Word daily to know him as well. I am not sure how my family would have ever made it without prayer. It kept us out of a lot of things that the enemy meant for bad on my family. But God! I remember my dad being in the hospital and the enemy tried his best to snatch the life out of him, but God wouldn't allow it to happen. God stepped in and turned it around and healed my daddy's body. God had other plans for my dad's life, and I am so glad about it because now he is pastoring a church again and continues to preach the Word. You can't negate prayer, no matter how hard you try to steer from it, life mishaps and situations would bring you right back to it. I know it did for me anyway and because of it, I am so blessed.

It didn't matter what was going on around my family, we sought God diligently. I mean, we would pray for the dog, cats, and the horses if we needed to and sometimes, we probably did. It didn't matter to us; we just wanted to have constant conversations with God to make sure he remembered our voices like mama said that he would. Talking about somebody who believed in the power of prayer, it was my family. Not only did they believe in prayer, but they could also get him on the line without any busy signals and no drop calls. We were raised in a Holiness church so that should tell you a lot right there. Holiness is living a devoted and righteous life unto God. Not everyone could have lived Holy and walked in my shoes during those times. However, out of all the teachings I received growing up, I still believe that Holiness is right. Sometimes it was very hard to uphold such standards and expectations while it seemed everyone was watching. Living a life of Christianity in the public eye, can be like a suicide watch, if you know what I mean. The way I viewed it at the same, it was very hard and unrewarding due to the pressure and judgmental attitudes we faced. I went through a lot of heartache in school just being the odd girl out. Often, I was embarrassed and humiliated because I did not act *normal* whatever that is. I mean, being teased, and bullied because of the way you dressed and acted were very hard for me. I would cry often and feel that I was targeted by others just because I was different. I believe that I was picked out to be picked on. God saw in me what I did not see in myself at the time. He saw that I had the ability and stamina needed to sustain myself through the hard times. We must learn to suffer and know that suffering is the will of God. It may not look or even sound profound, but it is. The bible tells us in James Chapter 1 to Count it all Joy when we fall into divers temptations. Saying that we should not be down and out when trials and tribulations hit our life, but we should rejoice and be glad in the Lord because the trying of our faith works patience. We cannot allow the enemy to get the Glory through our suffering so we must stand against our trials and know that everything will be alright. If we heed to the Will of God and know that he may not come when we want him to, but he is right on time, we can see the benefits of God's Glory if we hold out and persevere. Suffering says that I am build for the struggle and no weapon in hell can take me down. You must remember that suffering speaks. It allows God to see that we are willing to be broken because we understand the meaning of being broken and being put back together again with the same pieces. Although I did not understand it at the time, but I Thank God for using me as that broken piece. I do believe that God wanted me to help to teach others the importance of endurance. And if I had to do it all over again, I would. Living a life with standards and grace has taught me survival and has allowed me to become the woman I am today. And for that God, I am grateful.

The bible reminds us that we can do all things through Christ which strengthens us. This lets me know that no matter how difficult life situations and circumstances may come to weigh us down; we are already victorious in our fight. We must believe that God has already worked it out on our behalf and in our favor. God promised us that he would never leave us nor forsake us. We have to believe that because that is the Word of God. I totally believe that I am who I am now because God was who I needed him to be then. And he continues to be my strong tower and my provider especially when I needed him most. We must not fail him by giving up and throwing in the towel. That is too easy! Prayer is your weapon so use it. It is one of the few things that I know that can turn situations around in an instant. *Minute rice ain't got nothing on prayer.* Growing up, I use to always hear my mother say that prayer is the key and faith unlocks the door. Still today, I believe that with all of my beings because it has been proven to be so. Faith is the ultimate link to your blessing and to your breakthrough. A good example is shown in St. Matthew 17th Chapter where a man came to Jesus to heal his son who was a lunatic because the disciples were unable to cure the child. The bible said that Jesus rebuked the devil and the spirit departed out of the little boy within that same hour. This means that there was no hesitation or such, immediately healing came to the child. Why? Because Jesus had faith and he undoubtedly believed in his father and all we have to do is believe also. Later in the chapter, the disciples asked Jesus why they were not able to cure the child. Jesus then explained to them that they lacked faith. The disciples did not believe that prayer would heal the child. Without Faith it is impossible to please God. Without Faith it is impossible for your situations to change. We must believe that God can do anything but fail. The scripture also states in St. Matthew 17th Chapter that if you have faith as a grain of mustard seed, ye shall say unto this mountain, removes to yonder, and it shall remove. We have to remember that there is Power in our tongue and all we have to do is speak with our mouth and believe in our heart and immediately change shall take place.

In this moment, I don't know what you, your family, friends, and co-workers stand in the need of and the struggles that hold you down right now. I do know that we serve a God that is mighty and powerful to do exceedingly and abundantly above all that we could ask or think. We must rely on that power to change our situations and remove the chains that has oppressed us for so long and continues to hold us un bondage. So, today, I encourage you to allow God to do a work in you like never before. Allow him to permeate you through and through and without any refusals or rejections. It is up to you now to totally open and allow God full access to your inner man so that he can do what operations that needs to be done in you. In verse 21 of St. Matthew 17th Chapter Jesus states: Howbeit this kind goeth not out but by prayer and fasting. This has brought us right back and in full circle with the one and only…prayer. Prayer gives us reassurance that God can and will work it out again and again and again. It is up to us to take off the limits and let God be God.

Are you confident in the God that is within you? Philippians 1:6 says that being confident of this very thing, that he which hath begun a good work in you will perform it until the day of Jesus Christ. You have to believe in your heart; no matter what it looks like that the work has already begun in you. God has started planting the seeds in you and all you have to do is allow the seeds to grow and become the beautiful décor that God intended you to be. Sometimes, people may not see it or understand but just know God has the first and the last say about the gifts you are to walk in. It can be discouraging when others don't see your potential gifts and callings that God has gifted within you. This has caused many people to become stagnant in the house of God because of being judged by others. They feel that their gifts are no longer needed in the church. We are not put here to judge or be judged. The bible says that God is the only judge, and he is the only one who can judge us. I know that we have a few judgmental church goers that sit around in the house of the Lord and judge people's gifts. Often, they complain about what the people are not doing. These are the same people who are not going to do no more than what they are doing now which is little to nothing. They are set in their own ways and are against change. They have no desire to embrace the new things that God is doing in his churches on today. They are not about moving higher in God but staying where they are because that is where they find comfort. They see no need of changing how the worship service is being lead because it creates a comfortable atmosphere for them. These people are the ones who look you up and down and find everything that you do in church to be over the top. They are forever using the line, *"It Don't Take All of That"*. They refuse for their songs to be changed in the choir regardless of if the songs were sung 50 years ago, it is their safe haven. Remember these folks don't embrace change. They don't feel it is appropriate and necessary for the youth to have an explosion night and invite gospel rappers to perform because they feel this is *"worldly"*. Some of them are in my church and yours too. They have been there for a very long time doing the very same thing and in the very same positions. Oftentimes there are conflicts among themselves because of their battle with self-centeredness. They all fight for control and when they cannot get it among each other, they attack the congregation and the new saints. They refuse to *"fall back"* and give up their positions to the new congregants that join the church because they are afraid to be shown up due to their lacking. Don't forget these are the same folks you call deacon, usher, mother, sister, brother and first lady and pastor. When does the body of Christ learn the importance of growth in the House of God? In order for the church to grow, we must adapt and embrace CHANGE and move forward.

How do we get our churches to embrace change and move forward so that we can grow? First, we must pray without ceasing. Prayer is always the answer to any situation. The bible says when there are two or three gathered together and agreeing on the same thing, that he is in the midst. We have to believe that there is strength in numbers. When we learn to pull together then we can begin to see the Change and the Growth that we seek. For us to see the move of God's hands in our situation, we must get on one accord. One day, I was praying for my church and my church family, and I begin to thank God for the things that he had promised us, but I could not yet see. Because remember, Faith is not what we can see but what we cannot see. So, I wanted to trust God for what blessings he had already spoken over our church. At the time, I felt a strong sense to stand for the Body of Christ because I knew that God would keep his every Word. As I continued to pray and intercede for my church and church family, I heard God said to me.... "Mary, your emotions don't move me". Then he said, "Show Me Your Faith, and I Will Show You My Face". Now, I know God was not talking about his face per se but himself in the spirit. He was allowing me to know that if I had the Faith to believe in Him that he would stand up in our situation and show himself to be strong. One of my favorite scriptures comes from I John 15:7 that reads: If ye abide in me, and my words abide in you, ye shall ask what ye will, and it shall be done unto you. I have always stood by God in Prayer by seeking his face and trusting in his truth through the Word of God. I am even more convinced now that God is doing a new thing not only in me but in the Body of Christ as well.

You must search yourself and evaluate what you are doing to hinder the move of God in your church. Is it really leadership or could it be that you are the problem? Do you have a bad attitude and are negative about making changes and moving forward? God longs to shower us with his love and saturate the house of God with his Glory. However, God would like your invitation to come in and allow him to sup with you. Remember, God is a gentleman and not a burglar; therefore, he will not break in and disarm your alarm. However, he desires to sup with you, so he stands at your door knocking for you to let him in. I have been in the church all my life and have witnessed the seen and unseen but through it all one thing has always been consistent and that is Prayer changes things. I am a believer that a family that prays together, stays together.

Psalms 17:1-10 (KJV)

Hear the right, O LORD, attend unto my cry, give ear unto my prayer that goeth not out of feigned lips. Let my sentence come forth from thy presence; let thine eyes behold the things that are equal. Thou has proved mine heart; thou hast visited me in the night; thou has tried me, and shalt find nothing; I am purposed that my mouth shall not transgress. Concerning the works of men, by the word thy lips I have kept me from the paths of the destroyer. Hold up my goings in thy paths, that my footsteps slip not. I have called upon thee, for thou wilt hear me, O God: incline thine ear unto me, and hear my speech. Shew thy marvelous lovingkindness, O thou that savest by the right hand them which put their trust in thee from those that rise up against them. Keep me as the apple of the eye, hide me under the shadow of thy wings, from the wicked that oppress me, from my deadly enemies, who compass me about. They are enclosed in their own fat: with their mouth they speak proudly.